HOW A CHINESE AI STARTUP, DEEPSEEK, SHOOK THE WORLD
Deep Disruption

The Rise of Game-Changing Artificial Intelligence That Upended Big Tech and the Global Race

J. Andy Peters

Table of Contents

Introduction

The world has been captivated by the relentless march of artificial intelligence, a technological revolution that has redefined the boundaries of possibility. Over the past decade, AI has transformed from an experimental concept to a driving force shaping industries, economies, and even geopolitical strategies. Leading the charge are tech giants like OpenAI, Google, and Meta, each pouring billions of dollars into developing increasingly sophisticated AI models. These companies, backed by virtually limitless resources, have built sprawling data centers, harnessed enormous computational power, and employed some of the brightest minds on the planet. Their goal has been singular: to dominate the AI landscape and claim the top spot in what has become a high-stakes arms race.

But the story took an unexpected turn when a small Chinese startup, virtually unknown to the world, entered the arena. In an astonishingly short time, this company, DeepSeek, managed to upend the narrative entirely. With a model that costs a fraction of what their competitors have invested, they introduced a revolutionary approach to AI development. Their secret? Efficiency. While the established players focused on brute computational power and massive infrastructure, DeepSeek devised an algorithmic solution that was leaner, faster, and more cost-effective. Suddenly, the assumptions about what it takes to succeed in AI were called into question.

The implications of this breakthrough are profound. DeepSeek's emergence not only challenges the dominance of Western tech behemoths but also raises broader questions about the global balance of power in technology. If a startup with limited resources can achieve this level of success, what does that mean for the future of AI development? Could it signal a shift toward greater innovation outside traditional strongholds, or even a reimagining of how technological advancements are pursued? Beyond the world of tech, the ripple effects of this achievement could extend to markets, industries, and geopolitics, reshaping the global landscape in ways that are only beginning to be understood.

Chapter 1: The Market's Reaction to a Shocking Breakthrough

The morning the news broke about DeepSeek, the financial world was shaken to its core. The Nasdaq, known as the bellwether for the tech industry, plunged a staggering 600 points—a near three-percent drop in a single day. For seasoned investors, it was one of the most dramatic selloffs the tech-heavy index had seen in years, a visceral reaction to an announcement that few saw coming. The revelation of a small Chinese startup capable of achieving what many believed was only possible with billions in funding from Silicon Valley sent shockwaves through markets.

The selloff wasn't just a reflection of fear—it was a recalibration of expectations. Stocks tied to artificial intelligence, which had fueled much of the Nasdaq's meteoric rise in recent years, were hit the hardest. Companies like Nvidia, which dominates the GPU market essential for powering AI models, saw their shares tumble as investors began to question the sustainability of their growth. Big tech players, including Meta and Alphabet, faced similar downward pressure, their market values eroding in the face of a disruptive threat they had not accounted for.

The markets, typically a measure of confidence in future growth, suddenly found themselves in a state of uncertainty. What had been a soaring narrative of AI dominance by a select group of companies now faced a new twist. If DeepSeek could produce an AI model for a fraction of the cost, could it upend the competitive landscape entirely? Would the massive spending by Western tech giants be seen as unnecessary or even wasteful? These questions rippled through trading floors, prompting a scramble to reassess the fundamentals of the industry.

The shock wasn't limited to tech investors. Broader markets felt the tremor as well, with the Dow Jones Industrial Average and S&P 500 registering notable losses. Analysts were quick to point out that this wasn't just about one company's innovation—it was a paradigm shift. DeepSeek's emergence highlighted vulnerabilities in an industry that had been perceived as unassailable, shaking the confidence of those who had bet heavily on its continued dominance.

The announcement of DeepSeek's groundbreaking AI model sent ripples of uncertainty through the investment community, shaking the confidence of even the most bullish backers of tech giants. For years, companies like OpenAI, Google, and Meta had been heralded as untouchable leaders in artificial intelligence, buoyed by their immense financial resources, cutting-edge infrastructure, and monopolistic grip on the latest advancements. Investors had grown accustomed to the narrative that these tech behemoths would continue to dominate AI innovation, pouring billions into complex systems that required colossal data centers and computational power. This assumption had made tech stocks the crown jewels of modern portfolios.

But DeepSeek's sudden rise disrupted this carefully constructed narrative. Investors, who had watched these giants position themselves as the inevitable winners of the AI race, were now forced to reconsider whether the massive capital outlays that had driven their success were still justified. DeepSeek's AI model, reportedly developed for a mere $5.6 million, proved that innovation could thrive with far fewer resources. If this small Chinese startup could accomplish so much with so little, what did that say about the billion-dollar budgets and long development timelines of the industry's incumbents?

The resulting market volatility wasn't just about the shock of a new competitor; it was about the fragility of confidence in the tech sector's approach to AI. Companies like Nvidia, whose GPUs are critical to powering the large-scale models that OpenAI and others rely on, suddenly faced questions about the long-term demand for their products. If algorithmic efficiency could reduce reliance on massive computational power, what would that mean for Nvidia's dominance? Similarly, tech companies that had tethered their future growth to AI, from Alphabet's Google to Meta, saw their valuations dip as investors grew wary of whether these giants could adapt to the shifting landscape.

This shift in sentiment wasn't merely reactionary. Investors began to question the very foundation of their optimism about tech. Had the barriers to entry in AI been overestimated? Was the market's faith in high-cost innovation misplaced? For companies that had been riding the wave of AI-driven stock surges, this new reality was unsettling. The idea that a small, agile competitor could pose a legitimate threat to giants raised the specter of further disruption, leaving investors uncertain about where to place their bets in the rapidly evolving AI space. Confidence in the infallibility of tech giants had been shaken, and the reverberations were felt across portfolios worldwide.

For years, the narrative around artificial intelligence has been one of immense cost. The dominant belief was that innovation in AI required a staggering amount of money—billions of dollars spent on research, development, hardware, and energy. Companies like Meta, which announced plans to invest $65 billion into AI, and Anthropic, whose projects range from $100 million to as much as $1 billion per model, exemplified this approach. The scale of these investments became a symbol of both their commitment and their dominance, reinforcing the idea that only those with deep pockets could play in this field.

DeepSeek's emergence turned this assumption on its head. By claiming to have developed a competitive AI model for just $5.6 million, the Chinese startup challenged the very foundation of these strategies. Suddenly, the massive budgets touted by the likes of Meta and Anthropic seemed less like a strength and more like a vulnerability. If a small team with far fewer resources could create something this impactful, what was the justification for such colossal expenditures by the industry's biggest players? Investors and analysts alike began to question whether the AI arms race had been built on a foundation of inefficiency.

This wasn't just about money—it was about the methodology. Companies like OpenAI and Google had long operated on the premise that success in AI was tied to brute force computation: vast data centers, an insatiable demand for GPUs, and the processing of astronomical amounts of data. This approach had driven the industry's development but also created significant barriers to entry, ensuring that only a handful of corporations could compete. DeepSeek's model of algorithmic efficiency, which relied on smarter and leaner computation, suggested that innovation didn't have to be tied to brute force. It was a revolutionary idea, one that called into question the core of how AI had been developed up to this point.

The debate over sustainability quickly followed. The AI boom, after all, was predicated on the belief that high spending would lead to equally high returns. But what if that equation no longer held true? If smaller, more efficient models could perform at the same level—or better—than their resource-heavy counterparts, the entire economic framework of the AI industry would need to be re-evaluated. Companies like Meta, which had bet heavily on building massive infrastructure for AI, suddenly seemed less secure in their strategies. Would their investments still yield the returns they had projected, or would they find themselves outpaced by nimbler competitors?

The ripple effects extended beyond the tech world. The massive energy consumption tied to brute force computation—requiring data centers that devoured electricity at industrial scales—had long been a concern for environmentalists and governments.

DeepSeek's approach hinted at a more sustainable future for AI, one that could reduce the environmental footprint of technological progress. This added another layer to the discussion, as industry leaders scrambled to reconcile their strategies with the growing demand for efficiency and sustainability.

At its core, DeepSeek's model raised an uncomfortable but necessary question: Was the AI boom built on the wrong assumptions? As the debate unfolded, it became clear that the industry was at a crossroads, with the potential to reshape not only the future of technology but also the strategies of the world's most powerful corporations.

The announcement of DeepSeek's breakthrough sent waves through the technology and investment communities, sparking reactions from some of the most influential voices in the industry. Investors, analysts, and tech leaders scrambled to make sense of the development, their responses ranging from cautious optimism to outright astonishment. Among those captivated by DeepSeek's sudden rise was Marc Andreessen, a legendary tech investor and co-founder of Andreessen Horowitz, whose words carry significant weight in the industry. Andreessen didn't mince words when he described the achievement as "one of the most impressive breakthroughs" he had ever witnessed.

Andreessen's reaction encapsulated the awe many felt toward DeepSeek's ability to disrupt what had seemed like an insurmountable landscape dominated by Western tech giants. For an investor whose career has been defined by backing transformative technologies, such praise is rare and indicative of just how groundbreaking this moment was. His endorsement also highlighted the potential ripple effect of this disruption—how it might force a rethinking of investment strategies that had long been focused on brute computational power as the defining factor in AI success.

But Andreessen was far from the only one with strong opinions. Other key figures in the tech and investment worlds expressed varying degrees of amazement and skepticism. Some marveled at the efficiency of DeepSeek's model, which seemed to unlock a new frontier of innovation with far fewer resources than the industry had come to expect. The idea that a model could be trained for under $6 million while achieving results comparable to those requiring hundreds of millions sent shockwaves through boardrooms and trading floors alike.

However, not all reactions were celebratory. Skepticism ran high among some experts who questioned whether DeepSeek's claims could be independently verified. Was it truly possible to achieve such a leap in algorithmic efficiency, or was this a clever marketing ploy designed to inflate the company's value? This uncertainty didn't stop the markets from reacting, but it did inject a degree of caution into the optimism. For many investors, the prospect of such a disruptive force was both thrilling and unnerving—a reminder of the volatility that often accompanies technological breakthroughs.

Andreessen's statement, though, stood out as a rare moment of unfiltered admiration in an industry often marked by guarded praise. His confidence in the implications of DeepSeek's model reflected a broader sense that this was not just another competitor entering the AI race, but rather a potential inflection point in the way AI was developed and scaled. His words served as a rallying cry for those eager to embrace a future where innovation wasn't bound by massive budgets and infrastructural might but driven by creativity, efficiency, and bold thinking.

The weight of these investor voices added to the narrative surrounding DeepSeek. It wasn't just about what the company had achieved—it was about what their achievement represented for the broader AI ecosystem. Whether it signaled a new paradigm or simply a temporary shock, one thing was clear: the conversation around AI would never be the same again.

Chapter 2: The Birth of DeepSeek

DeepSeek's journey from obscurity to global recognition is a story that defies convention and reshapes expectations about innovation. Founded just over a year ago in China, this unassuming startup was hardly on anyone's radar. While the AI world fixated on the headline-grabbing achievements of OpenAI, Google, and Meta, DeepSeek quietly worked in the background, developing a vision that was both ambitious and unconventional. Their approach wasn't about building the largest data centers or using the most powerful hardware. Instead, it was about finding smarter, more efficient ways to train and deploy AI.

The turning point came with the release of their AI model, DeepSeek V3, a platform that challenged industry norms with its lightweight efficiency and surprising effectiveness. It didn't stop there. Shortly after, the company unveiled the reasoning engine R1, an open-source tool licensed under MIT, further disrupting the narrative. What made R1 remarkable wasn't just its capabilities—it was its accessibility. Anyone could download and post-train the model on modest hardware, including a standard laptop. This democratization of AI technology was unprecedented, signaling a shift away from the elite, resource-heavy operations that had dominated the space.

What propelled DeepSeek into the global spotlight, however, was its rapid rise on Apple's App Store. Within days of its public release, DeepSeek's app soared to the top, overtaking ChatGPT, a benchmark of mainstream AI success. The feat was as symbolic as it was impressive. ChatGPT had become a household name, backed by the immense resources of OpenAI, yet DeepSeek managed to eclipse it seemingly overnight. The implications were staggering: a small startup had not only caught up to a tech titan but had, in some ways, surpassed it.

This meteoric rise wasn't just a reflection of DeepSeek's technological prowess—it was a testament to the company's ability to meet user demands with a product that was both practical and groundbreaking. Unlike many AI tools that require powerful servers to operate effectively, DeepSeek's lightweight model offered unprecedented efficiency without compromising performance. For users, this meant seamless functionality at a fraction of the cost, and for competitors, it posed a direct challenge to the established order.

DeepSeek's success can also be traced to the ingenuity of its approach. By focusing on algorithmic efficiency rather than brute force computation, the company sidestepped the hardware limitations that often plague smaller developers. Restricted access to advanced chips due to geopolitical constraints might have been a setback for others, but for DeepSeek, it became an impetus for innovation. The result was a lean, scalable model that not only leveled the playing field but also shifted the rules of the game entirely.

From its humble beginnings to its dramatic entrance onto the global stage, DeepSeek's rise reflects the potential of bold thinking and disruptive innovation. In less than a year, it went from an unknown entity to a symbol of what's possible when ingenuity meets opportunity. Its trajectory is more than just a success story—it's a declaration that the AI landscape is no longer the exclusive domain of tech giants. The stage is now set for a new era, and DeepSeek has made it clear that it intends to play a leading role.

The claim that DeepSeek developed a cutting-edge AI model for just $5.6 million sent shockwaves through the industry. For years, the development of advanced AI models had been synonymous with astronomical budgets and infrastructure investments. Companies like OpenAI, Meta, and Anthropic had justified billion-dollar expenditures as the cost of staying at the forefront of the AI revolution. Against this backdrop, DeepSeek's achievement appeared almost miraculous—an innovation that rewrote the playbook on what it takes to build powerful AI.

To fully grasp the magnitude of this cost efficiency, one must first understand the scale of spending by the industry's major players. OpenAI, for example, required hundreds of millions of dollars to train its GPT models, relying on sprawling data centers and the most advanced GPUs available. Meta, with its ambitious AI agenda, projected an investment of $65 billion over several years, with much of that funding allocated toward building the computational infrastructure required to train and deploy large language models. Anthropic, another leading player, openly acknowledged spending between $100 million and $1 billion on its models, emphasizing the high costs associated with massive datasets and energy-intensive processing.

DeepSeek's $5.6 million achievement stood in stark contrast to this paradigm. The difference wasn't simply in the number; it was in the philosophy. While Western companies leaned on brute force computation—scaling up hardware and infrastructure to handle the demands of training complex models—DeepSeek opted for a more refined approach. By focusing on algorithmic efficiency, the company developed a system that minimized the computational resources required, drastically cutting costs without compromising performance.

The implications of this cost efficiency went far beyond mere budgetary concerns. DeepSeek's model demonstrated that innovation wasn't necessarily tied to financial might. Instead, it showed that creativity, ingenuity, and a willingness to challenge established norms could yield results that were not only competitive but transformative. The company's ability to run its models on modest hardware, even a laptop, further underscored the accessibility of its technology. It was a sharp departure from the norm, where advanced AI systems were often reserved for those with access to specialized infrastructure and millions of dollars in resources.

For the tech giants, DeepSeek's achievement raised uncomfortable questions. If a small startup could accomplish so much with so little, were their massive budgets truly justified? Could they maintain their dominance in a landscape where efficiency was proving to be as valuable as raw computational power? These questions loomed large as investors and analysts began to reevaluate the strategies that had driven the AI boom thus far.

But the significance of DeepSeek's cost efficiency wasn't limited to its impact on the tech giants. It also signaled a potential democratization of AI, where smaller players and emerging markets could enter the field without the previously prohibitive costs. This shift had the potential to unlock innovation on a global scale, introducing new voices and perspectives into the AI conversation.

Ultimately, DeepSeek's achievement served as a powerful reminder that technological progress doesn't always follow a linear path. By breaking away from the high-cost, high-infrastructure model that had dominated the industry, the company charted a new course—one that promised to reshape the future of AI and challenge the assumptions that had governed it for so long.

DeepSeek's lightweight AI model represents a dramatic shift in how artificial intelligence can be deployed and utilized. Unlike the massive, resource-intensive systems built by many Western tech giants, DeepSeek's innovation lies in its ability to achieve advanced functionality with a fraction of the computational requirements. This revolutionary approach not only cuts costs significantly but also makes AI technology far more accessible and practical for everyday use.

At the heart of this breakthrough is the company's emphasis on algorithmic efficiency—a focus on optimizing the underlying mathematical models rather than relying on brute computational force. Traditionally, large AI models have required vast amounts of computing power to process enormous datasets and train complex neural networks. This approach demands expensive GPUs, sprawling server farms, and enormous amounts of energy, resulting in costs that only the wealthiest companies can afford to shoulder. DeepSeek, however, challenged this notion by engineering a system that required far fewer resources to achieve similar, if not superior, outcomes.

This efficiency isn't just a theoretical advantage; it has real-world implications. DeepSeek's model can be run on relatively modest hardware, including laptops or smaller-scale servers, instead of the industrial-grade data centers that are typically required. By reducing the computational burden, DeepSeek has eliminated one of the largest cost drivers in AI development. Training and running an AI model no longer necessitate specialized chips or high-powered infrastructure, which are not only expensive but also require ongoing maintenance and consume significant amounts of energy.

For businesses and developers, this lightweight nature means greater flexibility. Instead of investing millions in hardware or relying on cloud-based solutions that charge hefty fees for compute power, companies can now run advanced AI applications locally. This reduces operating expenses while also offering more control over data and performance. Moreover, the ability to operate on smaller devices has far-reaching implications for industries that have been constrained by infrastructure limitations. Emerging markets, startups, and even individual developers can now access tools that were once out of reach, leveling the playing field in a way that seemed unthinkable just a few years ago.

The environmental benefits of this approach are also significant. Large data centers, which form the backbone of traditional AI systems, consume massive amounts of electricity and contribute to the tech industry's growing carbon footprint. By drastically reducing the need for such facilities, DeepSeek's model offers a more sustainable path forward, addressing one of the industry's most pressing concerns.

In essence, DeepSeek has redefined what is possible in AI by demonstrating that size and scale are no longer prerequisites for success. Its lightweight design isn't just a technical achievement—it's a paradigm shift. By proving that advanced AI can be both powerful and resource-efficient, DeepSeek has opened the door to a future where innovation is no longer limited by cost or infrastructure, but instead driven by creativity and ingenuity.

China's emergence as a significant force in artificial intelligence development is no accident. It stems from a unique combination of factors that have shaped the nation's approach to innovation. At the heart of this success is its deep and vast talent pool, a wellspring of skilled engineers, mathematicians, and computer scientists. This intellectual capital has given China the ability to compete in even the most cutting-edge fields, including AI, despite geopolitical challenges and resource constraints.

With a population of over 1.4 billion, China produces an extraordinary number of highly educated graduates each year, particularly in STEM fields. Universities across the country, backed by significant government investment, have churned out professionals who are not only well-trained but also motivated by the nation's drive to become a global technology leader. This sheer volume of talent creates a fertile environment for innovation, one that can rival or even surpass that of any other nation.

However, China's path to AI dominance has not been without its challenges. Western sanctions and export restrictions have limited the country's access to advanced chips and cutting-edge hardware, key components in the traditional AI development process. For many, this would have been a crippling blow, but for China, it became a catalyst for innovation. With no guaranteed access to the same resources enjoyed by Western tech giants, Chinese developers were forced to adopt an entirely different mindset. They couldn't rely on brute computational power; instead, they turned to algorithmic efficiency, focusing on smarter, leaner models that could deliver results without the need for massive infrastructure.

This constraint-driven creativity is at the core of DeepSeek's success. The company represents the epitome of China's adaptive ingenuity, designing systems that don't depend on the resource-intensive methods employed by companies like OpenAI or Google. By solving problems through more efficient algorithms rather than sheer hardware capacity, DeepSeek has showcased how necessity can fuel groundbreaking innovation. This approach isn't just a workaround—it's a redefinition of how artificial intelligence can be developed and deployed.

China's advantage also lies in its ability to operate on a scale few other nations can match. The country's vast population provides a wealth of data that can be leveraged to train AI systems, even with more efficient models. Moreover, the government's emphasis on technological self-reliance has created an ecosystem where companies are encouraged to push boundaries and innovate at all costs. DeepSeek, a product of this environment, reflects the culmination of these efforts—a company that has not only solved the immediate challenges it faced but also set a new benchmark for the global AI community.

In many ways, the constraints imposed on China have become a competitive edge. By fostering a culture of efficiency and resilience, these limitations have spurred advances that might not have been achieved under more favorable conditions. DeepSeek's lightweight, cost-effective model is a prime example of this phenomenon, demonstrating how the convergence of talent, necessity, and ambition can create something truly transformative. It's a powerful reminder that innovation often thrives not despite challenges, but because of them.

Chapter 3: Algorithmic Efficiency vs. Brute Force Computation

At the heart of DeepSeek's revolutionary breakthrough is a concept that has redefined the trajectory of artificial intelligence: algorithmic efficiency. This is the core innovation that sets DeepSeek apart from the industry's entrenched leaders. While traditional AI development has largely been synonymous with brute force computation—leveraging massive data centers, advanced GPUs, and staggering energy consumption—DeepSeek's approach challenges this paradigm entirely. It does so not by competing on size or scale but by innovating smarter, more streamlined methods to achieve the same or better results.

Algorithmic efficiency refers to the ability to optimize the underlying mathematical processes that power AI models, reducing the computational resources needed for training and operation. Rather than relying on sheer hardware power, DeepSeek's technology focuses on refining the algorithms themselves, finding more elegant and resourceful ways to process data and learn patterns. It's the equivalent of designing a high-performance car that achieves top speeds with a smaller, more efficient engine, rather than simply bolting on a bigger, heavier one.

This innovation is significant because it addresses some of the most pressing challenges in AI development. Traditional methods, like those employed by companies such as OpenAI or Meta, require vast amounts of computational power. These models are trained in massive data centers, where thousands of advanced GPUs run continuously, consuming enormous amounts of electricity. This approach not only drives up costs but also places a significant burden on the environment, as the energy demands of these operations rival those of small nations.

DeepSeek's model disrupts this status quo by proving that high performance doesn't have to come with high resource requirements. Its lightweight design allows it to run efficiently on modest hardware—laptops and smaller servers—without sacrificing functionality or accuracy. This challenges the assumption that bigger is always better in AI, showing that smarter algorithms can achieve similar results with far less computational power. By sidestepping the need for massive infrastructure, DeepSeek has effectively leveled the playing field, making advanced AI accessible to organizations and individuals that lack the resources of tech giants.

The implications of this approach extend far beyond cost savings. By reducing reliance on energy-intensive data centers, DeepSeek's technology offers a more sustainable alternative, addressing growing concerns about the environmental impact of AI. It also introduces a more decentralized model for innovation, where cutting-edge AI can be developed and deployed without the need for proprietary hardware or cloud-based services. This democratization of AI has the potential to unlock creativity and experimentation on a global scale, allowing smaller players and emerging markets to compete in a space that was previously dominated by a select few.

In challenging the brute force model, DeepSeek has sparked a broader conversation about the future of AI development. It raises critical questions about whether the industry's reliance on massive infrastructure is truly necessary or merely a byproduct of entrenched thinking. If smaller, more efficient models like DeepSeek's can achieve the same results, the entire foundation of the AI boom may need to be reevaluated. This shift in perspective is more than a technological advancement—it's a call to rethink how progress is measured, emphasizing ingenuity and efficiency over sheer scale. DeepSeek's innovation doesn't just change the game; it rewrites the rules entirely.

DeepSeek's revolutionary approach to artificial intelligence development poses a profound challenge to the traditional dynamics of the tech industry, particularly for companies like Nvidia, whose dominance in AI hardware has been largely unshaken—until now. Nvidia's GPUs have been indispensable for training and deploying large-scale AI models, and the company's growth has mirrored the explosion of AI demand. However, the disruptive nature of DeepSeek's algorithmic efficiency raises serious questions about the long-term relevance of brute-force computational methods, potentially reshaping Nvidia's role in the AI ecosystem.

For years, Nvidia's cutting-edge GPUs have been the backbone of the AI industry, relied upon by tech giants such as OpenAI, Google, and Meta to power their massive models. These chips, built for high-intensity parallel processing, are designed to handle the vast datasets and complex computations required for training neural networks. This hardware dependency has allowed Nvidia to maintain its dominance and demand premium pricing, as no viable alternatives existed for companies chasing AI supremacy. But DeepSeek's lightweight model introduces a paradigm shift. By optimizing algorithms to achieve more with less, DeepSeek reduces reliance on hardware-heavy solutions, suggesting that the need for high-end GPUs could decline over time.

If DeepSeek's model becomes a blueprint for future AI development, Nvidia's market dominance may face disruptions. A world in which advanced AI can be developed and run efficiently on consumer-grade hardware, such as laptops or modest servers, would challenge the necessity of Nvidia's high-performance GPUs for many applications. This could create ripple effects, forcing Nvidia to rethink its long-term strategies and adapt to a changing market where demand for brute-force computation is no longer the driving force of innovation. The implications are significant, as

Nvidia's growth has been heavily tied to the AI boom, and a shift toward lightweight models could dampen its revenue trajectory.

The impact isn't limited to Nvidia. The broader tech industry, particularly the operators of sprawling data centers, could also see major disruptions. Companies like Amazon, Microsoft, and Google, which run massive cloud computing platforms, rely on data centers to handle the computational needs of their AI services. These facilities consume enormous amounts of electricity, not only to power the servers but also to keep them cool in climates where temperatures can soar from the relentless heat generated by GPUs. DeepSeek's model, which operates with a fraction of the computational requirements, introduces the possibility of significantly reducing the energy demands associated with AI development and deployment.

This shift could have far-reaching environmental benefits. Energy consumption in data centers has been a growing concern, with their power usage rivaling that of entire countries. Reducing the reliance on energy-intensive infrastructure aligns with global calls for more sustainable practices in the tech industry. By cutting the energy requirements for AI, DeepSeek's approach not only lowers operational costs but also addresses the carbon footprint of AI at a time when environmental responsibility is becoming increasingly critical to corporate and governmental agendas.

For big tech, the implications of these changes go beyond cost and sustainability. They signal a broader need to adapt to an AI future that prioritizes efficiency over scale. Companies that have built their business models around the infrastructure-heavy demands of traditional AI may need to pivot, embracing algorithmic innovation to stay competitive. This could lead to a realignment of priorities within the tech ecosystem, as organizations reassess their investments in hardware, energy, and cloud services.

In the wake of DeepSeek's breakthrough, the question isn't just whether big tech can adapt—it's whether they can do so quickly enough to maintain their dominance in an industry that has been fundamentally reshaped. The disruption caused by DeepSeek represents both a challenge and an opportunity, forcing established players to innovate and evolve in ways that could redefine the future of technology.

The emergence of DeepSeek's innovative AI model has brought the tech world to a crossroads, presenting two distinct futures for the evolution of artificial intelligence. Each path carries profound implications for how technology is developed, deployed, and integrated into the global economy. At the center of this pivotal moment is a fundamental choice: will the industry embrace a world driven by algorithmic efficiency, or will it continue to rely on brute force computation?

In the first scenario, the future is shaped by algorithmic efficiency. This is the vision that

DeepSeek has introduced—a landscape where smarter, leaner models achieve comparable or even superior results with a fraction of the resources. In this world, AI development moves away from sprawling data centers and energy-hungry GPUs. Instead, lightweight models can run on modest hardware, democratizing access to cutting-edge technology. Smaller companies, startups, and even individual developers could participate in the AI revolution without needing the vast financial and computational resources currently required. The barriers to entry, which have long favored a handful of well-funded corporations, would be lowered significantly.

This path is not only more cost-effective but also aligns with growing concerns about sustainability. The reduced energy consumption of efficient models offers a way to address the environmental footprint of AI, mitigating the criticism that the industry has faced over its resource-intensive practices. It's a future where innovation is driven by creativity and ingenuity, not just capital and infrastructure, allowing for a more diverse and dynamic ecosystem.

The alternative future, however, sticks to the established course—a world dominated by brute force computation. This is the approach championed by tech giants like OpenAI, Meta, and Google, who have built their AI empires on the foundation of massive data centers, advanced GPUs, and unparalleled financial resources. In this scenario, the arms race for bigger, faster, and more powerful AI systems continues unabated. The focus remains on scaling up, pushing the limits of hardware and computation to create increasingly complex models.

While this approach has yielded groundbreaking advancements, it comes with significant trade-offs. The costs of development remain prohibitively high, limiting participation to a small number of companies. Energy consumption continues to soar, raising concerns about sustainability and environmental impact. Yet, for the major players, this path represents stability—it builds on their existing strengths and investments, leveraging their dominance in infrastructure and resources to maintain their competitive edge.

The stakes for global tech giants couldn't be higher. DeepSeek's breakthrough has introduced a disruptive force that threatens to upend the traditional paradigm. Companies that have poured billions into brute-force AI development now face a critical decision: pivot toward algorithmic efficiency or risk being outpaced by nimbler competitors. This isn't just a technological challenge; it's a strategic one. Pivoting would require rethinking core business models, reallocating resources, and embracing a mindset that values efficiency over scale.

For some, the shift may come too late. Entrenched in their existing methods, the biggest players may struggle to adapt quickly enough to keep pace with the innovations introduced by companies like

DeepSeek. Others, however, may seize the opportunity, leveraging their vast resources to refine and expand on the principles of algorithmic efficiency. The result could be a hybrid future, where the lessons of efficiency are integrated into the existing infrastructure, creating a new balance between power and precision.

Ultimately, the choice between these two futures will shape not just the trajectory of artificial intelligence but also the broader dynamics of the tech industry. It's a decision that carries profound implications for accessibility, sustainability, and innovation, with the potential to redefine what progress looks like in the digital age. Whether the world embraces efficiency or continues to rely on brute force, one thing is certain: the AI landscape will never be the same again.

Chapter 4: Global Implications of DeepSeek's Breakthrough

The emergence of DeepSeek has not only disrupted the technological and corporate landscape but also added a powerful new dimension to the geopolitical AI race. For years, the dominance of artificial intelligence innovation had been concentrated in the West, spearheaded by tech giants like OpenAI, Google, and Meta. These companies, backed by immense capital, cutting-edge infrastructure, and access to advanced hardware, have symbolized the United States' leadership in AI. However, DeepSeek's breakthrough has tilted the balance, positioning China as an even stronger competitor in this rapidly intensifying race.

China's rise in AI has been fueled by its government's strategic prioritization of technology as a cornerstone of national power. Unlike the West, where private corporations often drive innovation, China's AI ambitions are backed by state-led initiatives aimed at making the country the global leader in AI by 2030. DeepSeek's success exemplifies the effectiveness of this approach, demonstrating how China's combination of talent, resources, and necessity-driven innovation can produce disruptive advancements that rival and, in some cases, surpass the West's efforts.

DeepSeek's achievement sends a clear message: China is not merely catching up in the AI race—it is redefining the rules of competition. By focusing on algorithmic efficiency, the company has showcased an alternative path to dominance, one that circumvents the West's reliance on brute computational power and advanced hardware. Restricted access to Western chips and GPUs, which once seemed like an obstacle, has instead forced Chinese companies like DeepSeek to think creatively, leading to innovations that challenge long-held assumptions about the resources required for cutting-edge AI.

This development also signals a potential shift in global power dynamics. Western dominance in AI has largely been rooted in its control of advanced hardware, high-performance GPUs, and data center infrastructure. These assets, combined with significant capital, have created a seemingly insurmountable barrier for competitors. DeepSeek's success undermines this foundation, suggesting that leadership in AI may no longer depend on sheer resources but rather on ingenuity and efficiency. This levels the playing field, allowing emerging players and nations to compete in a way that was previously unimaginable.

For China, this breakthrough is more than just a technological milestone—it's a geopolitical advantage. AI is widely recognized as a critical tool for economic growth, military applications, and global influence. By demonstrating its ability to innovate independently of Western resources, China strengthens its position in a technology that is increasingly seen as a marker of national power. This shift could have far-reaching consequences, not only for the balance of technological leadership but also for how nations approach AI development as a strategic priority.

For the West, DeepSeek's success raises urgent questions. Can traditional models of AI development continue to dominate, or will the disruptive potential of algorithmic efficiency force a reevaluation of strategy? If nations like China can achieve global influence in AI with fewer resources, the Western monopoly on advanced technology could face significant erosion. This could lead to a more competitive global landscape, where innovation arises from diverse regions and players, rather than being concentrated in a few dominant hubs.

DeepSeek's rise is a wake-up call for the global AI community, signaling that the race is far from over and that the path to leadership may take forms that defy conventional expectations. As nations and corporations scramble to adapt to this new reality, the geopolitical AI race has entered a new phase—one defined not just by competition, but by the potential for a reshaping of global power itself.

The global reaction to DeepSeek's breakthrough has been a mixture of astonishment, skepticism, and unease. For a startup to achieve such a monumental advancement in artificial intelligence, particularly one with such low development costs and remarkable efficiency, was unexpected and disruptive. While some viewed it as a triumph of ingenuity, others approached the news with caution, raising questions about the validity of DeepSeek's claims and the broader implications of its emergence.

In the United States, analysts, policymakers, and industry leaders were quick to scrutinize the announcement. For an AI model to be developed for just $5.6 million—when competitors like OpenAI and Meta typically invest hundreds of millions, even billions, into similar projects—seemed almost too good to be true. Calls for independent verification of DeepSeek's results began almost immediately. Skeptics argued that the lack of transparency surrounding certain aspects of the development process left room for doubt. Could a model truly deliver such high performance with minimal computational costs, or was this an elaborate exaggeration? Until DeepSeek's claims were independently replicated, some warned against jumping to conclusions about the scope of its achievement.

Beyond technical scrutiny, the geopolitical implications of DeepSeek's success added an additional layer of concern. In the U.S., commentators likened this moment to the "Sputnik moment" of artificial intelligence—a technological leap from an unexpected competitor that could redefine global competition. Just as the Soviet Union's launch of the Sputnik satellite in 1957 had shocked the United States into accelerating its space program, DeepSeek's rise seemed poised to catalyze a similar reaction in AI development. The comparison reflected the anxiety that comes with recognizing that another nation—particularly China—has the potential to disrupt a domain traditionally dominated by the West.

Others took an even darker view, describing DeepSeek's emergence as a potential "Cyber Pearl Harbor." This metaphor painted the breakthrough as a strategic ambush, a reminder of how vulnerabilities in assumptions and complacency can be exploited to shift the balance of power. For decades, the U.S. and its allies have operated under the belief that their control of advanced hardware, infrastructure, and capital would ensure their dominance in AI. DeepSeek's success called those assumptions into question, sparking fears of a broader shift in technological leadership that could have far-reaching consequences for global security and economic stability.

Outside the U.S., reactions varied. In Europe, where governments have pushed for increased regulation of AI, DeepSeek's lightweight and efficient model raised questions about whether regulatory frameworks were prepared for such rapid advancements. Could existing oversight mechanisms adapt quickly enough to keep pace with the implications of disruptive innovation? Meanwhile, in other parts of the world, particularly in emerging markets, DeepSeek's approach was seen as an opportunity. The ability to develop and deploy powerful AI models without the need for expensive infrastructure offered a glimpse of a more accessible future, where advanced technology might no longer be the exclusive domain of wealthy nations and corporations.

Whether this moment will go down as a "Sputnik moment," a "Cyber Pearl Harbor," or simply an inflection point in AI history remains to be seen. What is clear, however, is that DeepSeek has sparked a wave of reflection and urgency across the globe. As stakeholders in government, industry, and academia grapple with the implications of this breakthrough, the AI community is being forced to reevaluate not just the strategies and assumptions that have defined its progress so far, but also the future trajectory of artificial intelligence on a global scale. The question is no longer whether the industry will change, but how quickly—and who will lead the way.

DeepSeek's rapid rise sent a jolt through global financial markets, triggering a reassessment of the underlying assumptions that had fueled the AI boom. For years, the narrative of AI dominance had been anchored in the seemingly unshakable strength of Western tech giants, whose massive investments in AI infrastructure and talent drove their market valuations to new heights. The emergence of DeepSeek, a relatively unknown Chinese startup with a radically efficient and low-cost approach, challenged that narrative and introduced an element of unpredictability that reshaped investor confidence.

At the heart of this shift was a question that rattled markets: had investors overestimated the value of massive AI budgets and hardware-intensive strategies? DeepSeek's ability to develop a competitive AI model for just $5.6 million cast doubt on the billions being spent by companies like Meta, OpenAI, and Google. These firms, once seen as unassailable leaders in the AI race, suddenly appeared vulnerable to disruption. For investors, this raised concerns about whether the returns on such heavy spending could justify the risks, especially if smaller, nimbler players like DeepSeek could achieve similar results with far fewer resources.

The ripple effects were immediate. Stocks in AI-related companies, particularly those tied to the infrastructure side of the industry, saw sharp declines. Nvidia, whose GPUs have been a cornerstone of AI training, faced significant downward pressure as investors questioned the long-term demand for its high-performance hardware. If algorithmic efficiency could reduce reliance on brute-force computation, the need for GPUs at the scale previously assumed might diminish, threatening Nvidia's dominant position. Similarly, cloud providers like Amazon, Microsoft, and Google, which host AI models in their energy-intensive data centers, faced questions about the future profitability of their AI-driven services.

Beyond specific companies, DeepSeek's rise signaled a broader reevaluation of investment strategies in AI. The traditional focus on funding companies with the largest budgets, infrastructure, and hardware access was no longer a guaranteed formula for success. Investors began to shift their attention to startups and innovators focused on efficiency, agility, and algorithmic breakthroughs. This marked a significant departure from the status quo, where resource-intensive approaches had dominated the narrative. DeepSeek's achievement suggested that the next wave of AI growth might come from companies capable of doing more with less—a trend that could open up new opportunities in underexplored markets.

The implications extended to venture capital as well. Investors who had previously focused on scaling existing giants began looking for smaller firms with disruptive potential, particularly those operating in regions outside the traditional tech hubs of the United States and Europe. Emerging markets, where access to large-scale infrastructure is limited, suddenly seemed like fertile ground for innovation. If DeepSeek could succeed with limited resources and restricted access to Western hardware, what other breakthroughs might be lurking in unexpected places?

For the broader market, the story of DeepSeek highlighted the volatility and uncertainty inherent in the AI industry. While the sector remains one of the most promising areas for growth, the emergence of new players and disruptive models has made it clear that the rules of the game are far from settled. Investors now face a more complex landscape, one where traditional metrics like spending and infrastructure may no longer be the primary indicators of success. Instead, the ability to adapt, innovate, and rethink established norms will likely define the winners of the next phase of AI development.

In the wake of DeepSeek's rise, the financial world is left grappling with a fundamental question: how much of the AI boom's valuation is built on solid ground, and how much is vulnerable to disruption? As investors recalibrate their strategies, one thing is certain: the confidence that once seemed so firmly rooted in the dominance of big tech has been shaken, creating a more dynamic—and unpredictable—market environment.

Chapter 5: The Future of Artificial Intelligence

DeepSeek's meteoric rise is a striking reminder of how quickly innovation can upend entire industries, particularly in a field as dynamic as artificial intelligence. In just over a year, a relatively obscure startup moved from conception to creating a breakthrough that disrupted some of the most entrenched players in the global tech landscape. This unprecedented pace of progress reflects the exponential acceleration of AI advancements, where transformative ideas and technologies are emerging faster than ever before.

AI, by its very nature, is a compounding force. Each advancement builds on the foundation of previous achievements, creating a cascade of progress that seems to defy traditional timelines. The release of large-scale language models like GPT set new benchmarks for what AI could achieve, but DeepSeek's success took the industry by surprise, showing that smaller, more efficient systems could challenge those benchmarks in a fraction of the time and at a fraction of the cost. What once required years of research and billions in investment now appeared attainable with a radically different approach.

This acceleration isn't happening in isolation—it is the result of several converging factors. The proliferation of open-source tools and research has democratized access to foundational knowledge, allowing smaller players like DeepSeek to innovate without starting from scratch. Collaborative efforts and publicly available frameworks have shortened development cycles, enabling startups to experiment and iterate at speeds unimaginable just a few years ago. DeepSeek's release of its reasoning engine R1 under an open-source MIT license is a continuation of this trend, amplifying the global pace of AI development.

Another driving force behind this rapid progress is the increasingly competitive nature of the AI landscape. As countries and companies race to gain an edge, the pressure to innovate has never been greater. The constraints faced by DeepSeek, such as limited access to advanced Western hardware, pushed the company to prioritize algorithmic efficiency, achieving results faster and with fewer resources. In doing so, DeepSeek exemplified how challenges can act as catalysts for breakthroughs, propelling innovation forward at an astonishing rate.

The implications of this rapid progress extend far beyond DeepSeek's individual success. It underscores a broader truth about the nature of technological revolutions: once a tipping point is reached, change occurs at an accelerating pace. What was once speculative quickly becomes mainstream, and new advancements emerge in rapid succession, building on each other to reshape industries and societies.

This speed of progress, however, also brings challenges. The industry must grapple with the ethical, regulatory, and economic implications of advancements that outpace traditional systems of oversight and adaptation. Governments, businesses, and institutions are now tasked with navigating a world where the next disruptive breakthrough could emerge virtually overnight. The pressure to keep up is immense, as the gap between those who lead and those who lag widens with each new innovation.

DeepSeek's story serves as a powerful reflection of how AI's acceleration can reshape the technological and economic landscape in record time. It is a reminder that in this new era, agility, creativity, and a willingness to challenge conventional norms are the keys to success. The pace of change is only accelerating, and the world is learning that the future doesn't just arrive gradually—it can appear all at once, propelled by the relentless momentum of human ingenuity.

DeepSeek's groundbreaking achievement carries profound implications for researchers, companies, and policymakers alike, forcing them to reassess their roles and strategies in the rapidly evolving world of artificial intelligence. As the pace of innovation accelerates and the barriers to entry for AI development lower, the ripple effects are reshaping priorities across the board, presenting both opportunities and challenges.

For researchers, DeepSeek's success is a wake-up call about the shifting dynamics of innovation. Traditionally, AI advancements have been driven by brute computational power, requiring vast resources and access to specialized hardware. DeepSeek's emphasis on algorithmic efficiency challenges this paradigm, opening the door for researchers to focus on smarter, more streamlined approaches. This shift encourages a reevaluation of priorities, placing greater emphasis on creativity and ingenuity rather than sheer scale. It also democratizes the field, allowing researchers in less resource-rich environments to make meaningful contributions without the need for immense infrastructure. However, it also demands a willingness to adapt quickly to new methodologies, as the industry's rapid evolution leaves little room for outdated practices.

For companies, particularly those that have invested heavily in infrastructure-intensive AI development, DeepSeek's breakthrough represents both a threat and an opportunity. On one hand, it raises uncomfortable questions about the sustainability of their current strategies. If algorithmic efficiency can deliver comparable results with significantly lower costs, companies reliant on brute force computation may find their models of growth and innovation increasingly vulnerable. On the other hand, the disruption also presents a chance to pivot and adapt. Forward-thinking companies can embrace efficiency-focused innovation, exploring how to integrate such approaches into their operations. Doing so could allow them to reduce costs, improve scalability, and remain competitive in a landscape that rewards agility over sheer size.

The implications for policymakers are equally significant. The rise of DeepSeek highlights the need for a new regulatory framework that can keep pace with the rapid acceleration of AI advancements. Traditional oversight mechanisms, designed for slower-moving industries, may no longer suffice in a world where transformative breakthroughs can emerge in months rather than years. Policymakers must navigate complex issues, such as the potential for economic displacement, the need for ethical standards, and the geopolitical implications of AI leadership. At the same time, they must balance regulation with the need to foster innovation, ensuring that overly restrictive policies do not stifle creativity and progress.

DeepSeek's success also underscores the importance of global collaboration and competition in AI. For policymakers, this means reevaluating national strategies to remain competitive in a more decentralized and democratized AI ecosystem. Investments in education, research, and innovation infrastructure will be critical, as will partnerships with emerging players who demonstrate disruptive potential. The geopolitical stakes are high, and countries that fail to adapt risk falling behind in a field that is increasingly central to economic and strategic power.

Ultimately, DeepSeek's rise signals a fundamental shift in how AI is developed, deployed, and integrated into society. Researchers, companies, and policymakers must all confront the reality that the traditional rules of the game no longer apply. Those who embrace change and prioritize agility, creativity, and collaboration will be best positioned to thrive in this new era of artificial intelligence. The challenge lies not just in keeping up but in actively shaping the future as it unfolds at an unprecedented pace.

DeepSeek's decision to make its R1 reasoning engine open source under the MIT license is a bold move that underscores the growing importance of transparency and collaboration in artificial intelligence development. By choosing to share its technology with the world, DeepSeek has signaled a commitment to fostering innovation beyond its own walls, opening the door for widespread adoption and unexpected advancements. This decision has implications that extend far beyond the company itself, shaping how AI evolves in an increasingly interconnected and collaborative ecosystem.

Open sourcing R1 means that anyone—researchers, developers, or even hobbyists—can access the technology, study its inner workings, and build upon it without restrictive licensing fees or proprietary barriers. This level of accessibility is transformative, especially in an industry often criticized for being controlled by a handful of well-funded corporations. By removing barriers to entry, DeepSeek has democratized access to advanced AI tools, empowering a new wave of innovators who may lack the resources of tech giants but possess the creativity and vision to contribute meaningfully to the field.

The choice of an MIT license further emphasizes DeepSeek's focus on fostering innovation. As one of the most permissive open-source licenses, it allows users to not only utilize the R1 model but also modify, improve, and even commercialize their versions of the technology. This level of flexibility encourages experimentation and diversification, as developers can adapt the model to suit a wide variety of applications, from industry-specific solutions to consumer-facing tools. In essence, it transforms R1 into a foundation upon which countless new ideas can be built, accelerating the pace of AI development globally.

Transparency plays a critical role in this process. By opening its model to scrutiny, DeepSeek invites the global community to test, validate, and enhance its technology. This collaborative approach can lead to faster improvements, as flaws and inefficiencies are identified and addressed by a wide range of contributors. Transparency also helps build trust, a crucial factor in a field often clouded by skepticism and concerns over opaque algorithms. With DeepSeek's decision, the company not only shares its achievements but also reinforces its credibility by showing confidence in its technology's robustness and value.

The ripple effects of this openness are profound. For organizations and developers in emerging markets, access to R1 could be a game-changer. Many of these regions lack the infrastructure and resources to develop their own advanced AI systems, but with R1, they gain a powerful tool that can be customized to address local challenges and opportunities. This democratization of technology has the potential to unleash a new wave of global innovation, where groundbreaking ideas emerge from unexpected corners of the world.

Moreover, DeepSeek's move could inspire other companies to adopt similar open-source strategies. As the benefits of collaboration become increasingly evident, the industry may shift toward a more open and interconnected approach to development.

While competition will always remain a driving force, the collective progress enabled by shared knowledge and resources could lead to breakthroughs that no single company could achieve alone.

Ultimately, DeepSeek's decision to make R1 open source reflects a forward-thinking vision of AI's future—one that prioritizes accessibility, collaboration, and transparency as essential components of progress. By inviting the world to participate in its innovation, DeepSeek has not only expanded the potential of its own technology but also set a powerful example for how the AI community can work together to shape a more inclusive and dynamic future.

While DeepSeek's achievements represent a major breakthrough in artificial intelligence, they also raise critical questions about the challenges that lie ahead for both the company and the broader AI community. Replicating DeepSeek's success and scaling its innovations to meet global demand will not be without obstacles. Meanwhile, the ongoing debate about the sustainability of traditional, high-cost AI development versus more efficient, low-cost models adds further complexity to the path forward.

One of the immediate challenges is whether DeepSeek's achievements can be consistently replicated on a broader scale. The company's ability to develop a cutting-edge AI model for just $5.6 million hinges on algorithmic efficiency—a novel approach that reduces reliance on expensive infrastructure and high-performance GPUs. While this efficiency is groundbreaking, scaling it to meet the diverse needs of industries and applications may introduce unforeseen complexities. Many AI models require customization and post-training to align with specific use cases, and maintaining this adaptability while keeping costs low could prove difficult.

Another potential roadblock is the broader ecosystem's readiness to adopt and integrate lightweight AI models. Industries that have built their workflows and infrastructures around traditional, resource-heavy AI systems may find it challenging to transition to a more efficient model. For example, companies heavily invested in large-scale data centers or reliant on GPU-heavy computing may resist changes that undermine the value of their existing investments. Overcoming this inertia will require both technical innovation and persuasive evidence that algorithmic efficiency can consistently outperform traditional methods.

DeepSeek itself faces significant challenges as it transitions from a disruptive startup to a global competitor. Maintaining its early momentum will require careful navigation of market pressures, competition, and potential geopolitical complications. While its lightweight, cost-effective approach has drawn attention, it must now demonstrate that this model can deliver consistent, scalable results across a wide range of applications. As DeepSeek's technology gains traction, it may also attract regulatory scrutiny, especially in regions where AI oversight is tightening. Ensuring compliance with emerging standards while preserving the accessibility and efficiency of its models will be a delicate balance.

On a broader level, the AI industry faces a pivotal debate about the sustainability of its current trajectory. For years, the dominant model of AI development has been one of brute-force computation, with tech giants like OpenAI, Meta, and Google pouring billions into massive data centers and advanced hardware. This approach has driven significant advancements but at a cost—both financially and environmentally. The energy demands of these systems have raised concerns about their long-term viability, particularly as global attention increasingly focuses on sustainability and climate impact.

DeepSeek's efficient, low-cost model presents an alternative that could address many of these concerns. However, the question remains: is algorithmic efficiency a universal solution or simply one approach among many? Large-scale AI systems still have advantages in certain areas, particularly in tasks requiring immense computational capacity or highly specialized training. The future of AI may not be a simple choice between high-cost and low-cost models but rather a convergence of both approaches, where efficiency and scale coexist to address different needs.

For the AI community, these challenges represent an opportunity for introspection and adaptation. Researchers will need to explore how to further optimize algorithmic efficiency while addressing its limitations. Companies must decide whether to pivot toward more sustainable practices or double down on their existing methods. Policymakers will need to balance regulation with support for innovation, ensuring that new models of AI development can thrive without compromising ethical and environmental standards.

In many ways, DeepSeek's rise is a microcosm of the larger questions facing the AI industry. It highlights the potential for transformative change while underscoring the complexity of navigating an increasingly dynamic and competitive landscape. The challenges ahead are significant, but they also present a chance for the industry to redefine itself, embracing a future that values creativity, sustainability, and inclusivity as much as technological achievement.

Conclusion

DeepSeek's emergence stands as a defining moment in the evolution of artificial intelligence—a breakthrough that challenged long-held assumptions about what it takes to achieve innovation in one of the world's most competitive industries. By prioritizing algorithmic efficiency over brute force computation, DeepSeek disrupted the status quo, proving that smaller, leaner models could rival, and in some cases surpass, the results of resource-heavy systems built by industry giants. This paradigm shift has reshaped the conversation around AI development, forcing companies, researchers, and policymakers to reevaluate the principles that underpin the field.

At its core, DeepSeek's rise underscores the transformative power of thinking differently. In an industry dominated by massive budgets, sprawling data centers, and high-performance hardware, the company demonstrated that creativity and ingenuity could overcome even the most daunting constraints. Its success is a testament to the value of questioning established norms and exploring alternative paths, a lesson that resonates far beyond AI. For Western companies, this moment serves as a wake-up call—a reminder that dominance in technology cannot be taken for granted and that agility, adaptability, and efficiency are just as critical as scale and resources.

The road ahead for the AI industry is both uncertain and filled with opportunity. DeepSeek's breakthrough has accelerated the pace of competition, opening the door for new players to enter the field and challenging existing leaders to innovate at a faster rate. The industry now stands at a crossroads, with the potential for global collaboration and competition to drive unprecedented advancements. As algorithmic efficiency becomes a more central focus, the barriers to AI development are lowering, allowing innovation to emerge from unexpected places and introducing voices that were previously excluded from the conversation.

Yet this future is not without its challenges. The rapid acceleration of AI progress raises questions about regulation, ethics, and sustainability, requiring careful navigation by all stakeholders involved. Companies and governments must balance the drive for innovation with the responsibility to ensure that AI serves the greater good, addressing societal needs while mitigating risks. Collaboration between nations, industries, and research communities will be essential to harness the full potential of AI while ensuring it remains accessible and equitable.

DeepSeek's journey is a reminder that the future of AI is not set in stone. It is a story of how bold ideas, even from the most unexpected sources, can redefine what is possible and inspire an entire industry to think differently. As the AI arms race continues, the focus must shift toward fostering creativity, embracing efficiency, and building a collaborative ecosystem where innovation can thrive. The world is on the cusp of a new era in artificial intelligence—one shaped by uncertainty, opportunity, and the relentless pursuit of progress. In this landscape, the lessons of DeepSeek will resonate as a guide for navigating the challenges and seizing the possibilities of the future.

www.ingramcontent.com/pod-product-compliance
Lightning Source LLC
LaVergne TN
LVHW052128070326
832902LV00039B/4497